W9-BLV-384

# Vol. 50, No. 1

**Publisher**, Patricia A. Pingry
**Associate Editor**, Tim Hamling
**Art Director**, Patrick McRae
**Contributing Editors**, Lansing Christman, Deana Deck, Russ Flint, Carol Heyer, Pamela Kennedy, Heidi King, D. Fran Morley, Nancy Skarmeas
**Editorial Asst.**, Donna Sigalos Budjenska

ISBN 0-8249-1106-7
IDEALS—Vol. 50, No. 1 February MCMXCIII IDEALS (ISSN 0019 -137X) is published eight times a year February, March, May, June, August, September, November, December by IDEALS PUBLISHING CORPORATION, P.O. Box 148000, Nashville, TN 37214 Second-class postage paid at Nashville, Tennessee, and additional mailing offices. Copyright © MCMXCII by IDEALS PUBLISHING CORPORATION. Printed and bound in the United States. POSTMASTER: Send address changes to Ideals, Post Office Box 148000, Nashville, Tenn. 37214-8000. All rights reserved. Title IDEALS registered U.S. Patent Office.

SINGLE ISSUE—$4.95
ONE-YEAR SUBSCRIPTION—eight consecutive issues as published—$19.95
TWO-YEAR SUBSCRIPTION—sixteen consecutive issues as published—$35.95
Outside U.S.A., add $6.00 per subscription year for postage and handling.

### ACKNOWLEDGMENTS

A CUP OF TEA by Edgar A. Guest from *THE PASSING THRONG*, copyright © 1923 by The Reilly and Lee Co. Used by permission of the author's estate. WINTER ROAD from *THE GOLDEN ROAD* by Edna Jaques, copyright © in Canada by Thomas Allen & Son Limited. Our Sincere Thanks to the following authors whom we were unable to contact: Violet Rourke Broderick for THE FARM IN WINTER; Margaret Freer for SMALL BOY DILEMMA; Blanche McCauley Hallett for FEBRUARY SAYS GOODBYE; Brian King for ICE DANCE; Doris Van Owen for FAIRY FOOTPRINTS; May Smith White for TREASURED THINGS; and Carice Williams for THE KEY OF LOVE.

Four-color separations by Rayson Films, Inc., Waukesha, Wisconsin.

Printing by The Banta Company, Menasha, Wisconsin. Printed on Weyerhauser Lynx.

The paper used in this publication meets the minimum requirements of American National Standard for Information Sciences—Permanence of Paper for Printed Library Materials, ANSI Z39.48-1984.

Unsolicited manuscripts will not be returned without a self-addressed stamped envelope.

Cover Photo
H. Armstrong Roberts

Inside Covers
Gerald Koser

# Winter Morning

Edna Jaques

A morning crisp as watered silk,
With blankets of new fallen snow
Tucking the little houses in
For fear their naked feet will show.
The trees and shrubs are beautiful
Wrapped in their coats of carded wool.

The children on their way to school
In knitted caps and scarlet coats
Play hide and seek behind the drifts;
Their laughter rises high and floats
Above the highest maple tree
Like half forgotten melodies.

The shop where mother buys the bread
Has glittering panes of frosted glass
Through which the lights take on a glow
Like holy candles at a mass.
The streets are paved with softest down
As if a king had come to town.

A sleigh goes by with chiming bells,
Young people riding for a lark;
Their merry voices seem to ring
With extra sweetness in the dark
As if they tasted suddenly
How lovely simple things can be.

When Earth puts on her ermine wrap
And holds white diamonds in her lap.

# Fresh Snowfall

Kay Hoffman

A fresh snowfall in winter
Always brings my heart delight
When I waken in the morning
To a wonderland of white.

No pathway leading here or there
To mark the hurried pace,
Just fragile etchings in the snow
That wayward branches trace.

How cozy rests each little home
Knee-deep in drifts of snow;
Smoke curling up from chimneys
Adds to the friendly glow.

Fir trees don a regal look
In lavish ermine wrap;
Lamp posts, too, wear winter's best,
White muffler and top hat.

Our little town so peaceful is
A wonderland of white,
A picture postcard sent from God
To bring our hearts delight.

Photo Opposite
VILLAGE SNOW
Waits River, Vermont
William Johnson
Johnson's Photography

# Winter Countryside

Elisabeth Weaver Winstead

A white-feathered snow has fallen
And covered the faded green,
As I make fresh, fragile footprints
In the snow-shimmered country scene.

As I walk the lane through winter
With gold autumn past and gone,
The world lies silver-spindled
In the ice-crystal, country dawn.

The singing brook is silent,
Frozen firm in winter's clasp,
Hemmed in frost-laced stitchery
With ice-laden blades of grass.

The winter world is a sparkling land;
Trees glisten in sequined artistry.
Each dazzling crystal's wind-spun design
Is ablaze with diamonds for all to see.

WHITE WONDERLAND
Oak Creek Canyon, Arizona
Bob Clemenz Photography

# Winter Wonder

Sister Mary Lenore Baader

Who painted this landscape during the night
With beautiful pictures of silvery white—
Of bushes and trees and frosted lakes,
Of sparkling stars and starry snowflakes?

And what a surprise, a lovely surprise!
The dazzling, pure snow, to wondering eyes,
Blanketing softly the cold, bare earth.
To silent beauty, winter gave birth!

Photo Opposite
MOUNTAIN SNOWSCAPE
Buena Vista, Colorado
Grant Heilman
Grant Heilman Photography

# Ice Dance

Brian F. King

The pine trees stand by lakes of light
That mirror sunbeams shining bright.
The ice-locked waters gleam and glow
Like jewels set in crowns of snow,
And skaters waltz and pirouette
In sun-splashed pools of frozen jet.

**10**

Now side by side the skaters whirl,
The laughing boy, the graceful girl;
And velvet shadows fast retreat
Before their flashing, bladed feet.
And bonfires blaze to warm and thrill
The watchful, silent, snow-capped hills.

Like figures in a gay ballet,
The darting skaters swirl and sway
And dip and glide and bend and wheel
On sparkling blades of polished steel,
While swaying pines along the shore
With branches green applaud for more.

# The Farm in Winter

Violet Rourke Broderick

Feathered clouds of snow-white float
    In winter's noonday sky;
The gentle hills illumined by
    The sunlight rising high.

Snowdrifts blanket furrowed earth
    And hug the old, red barn;
Pines are decked with icy fringe
    And sugar-glaced, the tarn.

The winding farm road's muffled;
    The earth seems standing still,
Except when sounds of footfalls
    Echo in the frosty chill.

WINTER FARM
Nestlebrook Farm, New Hampshire
Dianne Dietrich Leis, Photographer

# Winter Night

Stella Craft Tremble

Give me a book and a fireplace
On a cold and starry night,
While I'm warm and cozy by the fire
And the world is ermine white.
The puff and crackle of the blaze
Is a welcome sound to hear,
And a place beside the fire I love
When the night is cold and clear.

Let biting winds that whip the snow
Lash the leafless trees about.
Let the creaking branches bend below
The weight of the sleet without.
Let Winter hold in her icy clasp
The snowdrifts mounting high;
I'll sit by the window undisturbed
By the storm that passes by.

Here at home is a happy coign
Where winter is held at bay;
From flaming tongues of the ruddy fire
Come songs of a summer day.
Let the full, round moon that's riding
High into my window stare;
I'm cozy at home before the fire
And heaven is with me there.

Photo Opposite
FIRESIDE WARMTH
Jessie Walker Associates

# Winter Night

Mary F. Butts

Blow, wind, blow!
Drift the flying snow!
Send it twirling, whirling overhead!
There's a bedroom in a tree
Where, snug as snug can be,
The squirrel nests in his cosey bed.

Shriek, wind, shriek!
Make the branches creak!
Battle with the boughs till break o' day!
In a snow cave warm and tight,
Through the icy winter night,
The rabbit sleeps the peaceful hours away.

Call, wind, call!
In entry and in hall!
Straight from off the mountain white and wild!
Soft purrs the pussy-cat
On her little fluffy mat,
And beside her nestles close her furry child.

Scold, wind, scold!
So bitter and so bold!
Shake the windows with your tap, tap, tap!
With half-shut, dreamy eyes,
The drowsy baby lies
Cuddled closely in his mother's lap.

# Readers' Reflections

*Editor's note*:

Readers are invited to submit unpublished, original poetry for possible publication in future issues of *Ideals*. Please send copies only; manuscripts will not be returned. Writers receive $10 for each published submission. Send material to "Readers' Reflections," Ideals Publishing Corporation, P.O. Box 140300, Nashville, TN 37214-0300.

## Pledge of Love

Let nothing come between us
To make each other sad.
Let nothing come between us
And lose just what we have.

I pray that I will never
Do anything at all
To make you want to lose me
From winter until fall.

You know I love you dearly;
You are my life to me.
You know that I will clearly
Do my best to make you see

That always I will love you
Through anything at all.
Just wait and I will show you
I am worthy of the call.

I will be with you in sickness,
In happiness and health,
And, if God is willing,
In riches and in wealth.

All these things I promise
To give to you, and then
I will wake up in the morning
To start it all again.

William C. Dragosavac
Pickens, South Carolina

18

## Winter World

Winter is a glorious time;
There is brilliance all around—
Icicles gleaming from the eaves
While snow glistens on the ground.

Yes, winter brightens up our lives
With its overcoat of white.
It's fun to walk in snow by day
And gaze out at it by night.

The winter world is like a movie
With scenes forever changing;
Where once snow made specific views,
Now the snow is rearranging.

We know that soon all this will end,
Into spring we'll soon reenter;
But our thoughts and hopes carry on
To next year's world of winter.

> Floy Wallace
> Des Moines, Washington

## For One I Love

May you wake to the glory
Of a roseate dawn—
A soft martin trilling
That night is gone.

May you walk in the sunlight,
No clouds in the blue!
Joy, your companion,
To walk with you.

May you run with the wings
Of a light-hearted breeze
And rest in the shadow
Of sheltering trees.

Then dream, if you will,
With the setting sun,
Of my love never ending
When day is done.

> Mary Peacock
> Cherry Hill, New Jersey

# Love's Philosophy

Percy Bysshe Shelley

The fountains mingle with the river,
    And the rivers with the ocean;
The winds of heaven mix forever
    With a sweet emotion;
Nothing in the world is single;
    All things by a law divine
In one another's being mingle:
    Why not I with thine?

See! the mountains kiss high heaven,
    And the waves clasp one another;
No sister flower would be forgiven
    If it disdained its brother;
And the sunlight clasps the earth,
    And moonbeams kiss the sea:
What are all these kissings worth,
    If thou kiss not me?

SNOW-COVERED CAPITOL BUTTE
Sedona, Arizona
Bob Clemenz Photography

# Winter Rose

John C. Bonser

My love is like a winter rose,
Her beauty blooming still,
Though time's relentless river flows
And frost lies on the hill.

My love is like an evergreen,
Bright-leafed against the snow;
Though autumn's flame has left the scene,
The ashes softly glow.

My love is like a treasured song
That ever sweeter grows;
My heart, with gladness, sings along
Though years the rhythm slows.

My love is like a photograph
Of one whose gracious pose
And gentle ways and happy laugh
The camera's magic shows.

My love is like the precious grain
In spring a farmer sows,
Till kissed by sun and wind and rain
To golden ripeness grows.

My love is like a dear old friend
So wonderful to know;
Upon life's path, from end to end,
Together we will go.

My love is like a winter rose
That frost can never kill;
In memory's soil her goodness grows
And beauty blossoms still.

VALENTINE TREASURES
Ralph Luedtke, Photographer

# Works of Love

Dorothy Bettencourt Elfstrom

If I can sprinkle seeds of joy
On someone's barren plot
And bring to light some cause for hope
That he has long forgot;

If I can lighten someone's load
That seems too great to bear,
Assuring him his fellow man
Is not too rushed to care;

If I can help renew one faith—
Restoring someone's smile,
My life will be enriched to seem
A little more worthwhile.

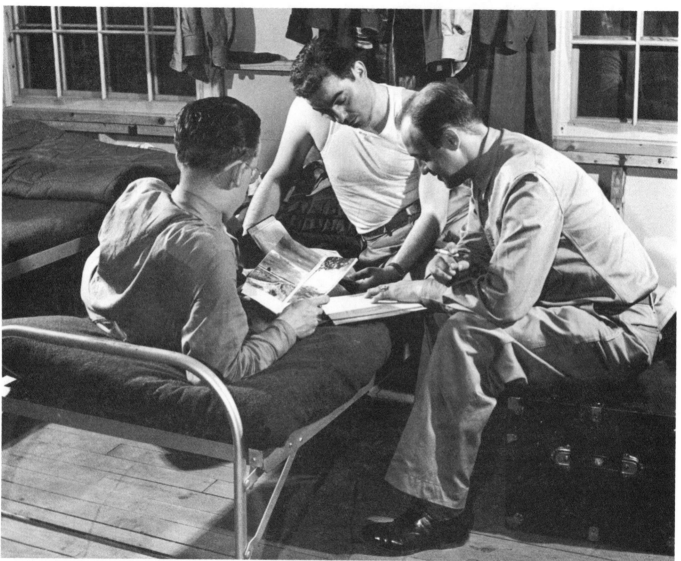

Archive Photos/Ben Schnall

## Books and Soldiers

The American soldier, with an inherent love of reading and a boundless curiosity concerning things and events, is making wide use of library facilities provided in and near military camps, and has hailed with satisfaction the nationwide move to collect books and expand these services.

Every military establishment where there are more than 5,000 men has its own library and attendants, under the direction of the branch of the service to which it belongs. Library service among the armed forces even extends to the detachment of men leaving for an isolated post. Each man is asked to include one volume among his personal effects, thus making a library of as many volumes as there are men.

Various organizations, dedicated wholly or in part to the maintenance of morale, have provided books, magazines, and reading facilities for the use of soldiers and sailors throughout the country. Thousands of books have been gathered, cleaned, mended, and repaired by the Work Projects Administration for distribution to military establishments.

The WPA Library Service Program for several years directed its activities toward bringing books and library facilities to those rural and isolated sections of the country where a varied collection of books was a rarity. The activities of the unit continued on this line until the advent of defense activities, when it was directed into the channel of providing books and library workers in training camps. Now, with the full war activity in swing, the program has been redirected so that in every place where the service libraries are not operating—in service centers in many towns, in lounging rooms in rail terminals, in branch libraries in many camps and other places where library aid has been requested—the WPA Library Program has stepped in with a trained staff and performed the necessary work.

To further the supply of books, a "Victory Book" campaign was initiated in January, in which the American Library Association, the Red Cross, United Service Organizations and kindred agencies sought to find 1,000,000 volumes, and with the aid of the WPA collect, sort, clean, mend, and distribute them to camps all over the country.

Titles available in the larger libraries not only range through the whole realm of fiction, but include a goodly number of books on other subjects. The camp librarians report that fiction requested is almost all of high grade.

Volumes dealing with pure science—chemistry, physics, and mathematics—are much in demand. Books on applied science—engineering, aviation, agriculture, mechanics, medicine, and hygiene—are popular. Biography, travel, history and languages are asked for often. The social sciences—economics, law, government, education and commerce—are also in demand. There is large demand for books on the Bible, poetry, gen-

Archive Photos/Jay Florian Mitchell

eral literature and drama.

The service seems to feel that an informed soldiery will be an intelligent soldiery, better able to carry out details and assignments because it knows the ideals it is fighting for. Instead of trying to mold the youth of the nation into a strict, military pattern, commanders of both the Army and Navy are encouraging the use of books, of studying and reading, knowing that an educated and thinking citizen soldiery will be more aware of all that it is fighting for.

Originally printed in *The Christian Science Monitor Magazine*, February 28, 1943.

# Treasured Things

May Smith White

I love old glass and roses too;
Each somehow seems to warm my soul.


To place pink roses in glass of blue
Fills my heart with thoughts of you.


I like to watch the sunset's hue,
Its rays against the crystal bowl.


I love old glass and roses too;
Each somehow seems to warm my soul.

# COLLECTOR'S CORNER

D. Fran Morley

## Collecting Depression Glass

Following World War I, glass manufacturers throughout Pennsylvania, West Virginia, and the Midwest began producing mass quantities of inexpensive, machine-pressed glass that was sold in five-and-dime stores or given away as promotional inducements for other products. Because it was first mass produced from the 1920s to 1940s, the glassware became known as Depression glass. Patterns and styles, however, were often reissued in the 1950s and 1960s. Now, the term Depression glass encompasses both glassware made during the era of the Great Depression and glassware made in particular patterns and styles.

Depression glass, like other pressed glass, is shaped by molds in machines. The pattern can be felt on the outside of the glassware; the inside should be smooth to the touch. The edges of Depression glass and other pressed glass should be blunt. In contrast, the edges of cut glass will feel sharp.

Depression glass can be either opaque or transparent. Popular opaque colors include medium blue, white, off-white, jade green, and yellow. Transparent colors include crystal, amethyst, cobalt blue, amber, green, and pink. Those who collect a certain color might include vases, tumblers, dessert plates, canisters, and serving bowls in various patterns, but all will be transparent pink or green or opaque white. Collectors will be very specific as to why "their" color is the best to collect and will usually refer to their collections as simply "green glass" or "pink glass."

Collecting by item can be fun and can still offer the collector plenty of variety. The typical set of Depression glass included a sherbet dish, salad plate, bread and butter plate, cup and saucer, cake plate, dinner plate, soup cup, and luncheon plate. Tumblers were much more prevalent than stemmed glassware, such as wine glasses, because Prohibition remained in effect nationally until 1933.

Pink glass from the author's collection.
Photography by Bob Schwalb.

The era also affected the production of glassware in other ways. As refrigerators became more widely used and the manufacturers began to advertise glass as a clean, hygenic method of food storage, special storage pieces such as butter dishes and ice-box pitchers were produced. Other popular items included canisters, salt and pepper shakers, juice reamers, and measuring cups. Many choose to begin collections with these pieces, but others collect by specific pattern designs.

Collecting by pattern involves the most research and can be very difficult. The variety of patterns made was enormous; just a few of the names include Daisy, Petal Swirl, Crisscross, Patrician, Moderntone, Circle, Mayfair, Pansy, Cube, Bubble, and Honeycomb. Often patterns would resemble each other even though they were made by a different company. To compound the problem, patterns were often reissued in later years. These second editions could be heavier or lighter in weight or lighter or darker in color than the original. Fortunately, many of the companies that produced Depression glass in the 1920s, such as Anchor-Hocking, Federal Glass, and Indiana Glass, are still producing glassware. Contacting these companies is the best method of dating and identifying a pattern as an original first edition or a reissue.

Since Depression glass was introduced in massive quantities to be used as functional glassware, abundant amounts of it can be found today. Families who passed their pieces on to future generations provided an excellent base for beginning a collection. Ironically, the abundance of Depression glass has worked against it as a collectible. Thousands of collectors now comb auctions and yard sales for specific pieces to add to their collections.

The increased demand has limited the supply and raised the price of many pieces. Some patterns in a particular color and pattern can be difficult to find. For example, an orange reamer in the Crisscross pattern might sell for ten dollars in crystal or green but is worth around two hundred dollars in blue or pink. A piece that just a few years ago could be purchased for a dollar is now being sold for ten or twenty dollars at antique stores. Even if real bargains are gone, however, most pieces are still reasonably priced and well within any budget.

A collector of Depression glass has to remember that most of the pieces were kitchenware and received regular use in homes. Consequently, bowls might be missing lids or plates might have surface scratches. This type of damage may not affect the sentimental value of an item, but it may affect the monetary value. Cracks and chips, of course, are different. If the collector considers the piece an investment, any crack or chip is unacceptable.

Many Depression glass collectors are looking for pretty or unusual pieces, not for investments. As with all collectibles, a collector should choose pieces that have personal appeal. An inherited vase with a tiny chip on the bottom might have low value as an investment; but if it is filled with pretty spring flowers and placed on a tabletop, its personal value can be priceless. A vase such as this can be the perfect piece to begin a lovely collection of Depression glass.

Jadite bowl and opaque shakers
from the author's collection.
Photography by Bob Schwalb.

# Key of Love

Carice Williams

In every happy home there is
    A special golden key
That opens up the doors of love,
    Of joy, and harmony.

Without this key you only have
    A pile of wood and stone.
It soon transforms a house to home,
    A chair into a throne.

This golden key lets in the sun
    And makes every corner sing;
He who holds the key of love
    Can open anything.

Photo Opposite
VICTORIAN PARLOR
Jessie Walker Associates

# Country CHRONICLE

—— Lansing Christman ——

Let the February snows come. Years ago when I lived in upstate New York, we had ample snows every winter. I like to remember certain phases of those old-fashioned winters. Christmas was always special, but as a youngster in the little country school, I looked forward to another special time—a snow for Valentine's Day.

Throughout the winter, we would sled down hills, build snowmen and forts, and dig caves in huge banks that came with blizzard-like winds. On February 14th, during our noon recess from class, many of us would make what we called "valentine hearts" in the snow. We would pick an old meadow nearby, one blanketed in white, and there we would walk in such a pattern

that our footprints would leave those heart-shaped figures of love.

Among the players were both boys and girls. After a heart was formed, a boy would use a long stick to inscribe in the snow the initials of a girl he thought was especially pretty or cute. A girl, of course, would inscribe in her heart the initials of her favorite boy in the class.

Here in upstate South Carolina, my home for the past twenty-three years, snows are not that common. When there is snow, the young bring out their sleds. They build snowmen and their forts and caves; but even when there is a land of white,

I have yet to see those images of hearts traced in the snow.

I have watched with pleasure, however, as a boy and girl walked hand in hand, or arm in arm, after a Carolina snow, leaving little need to create those hearts in a meadow of white somewhere. Their walk, either under the sun or under the stars, was their cherished valentine of love.

*The author of two published books, Lansing Christman has been contributing to* Ideals *for almost twenty years. Mr. Christman has also been published in several American, foreign, and braille anthologies. He lives in rural South Carolina.*

# Fairy Footprints

Doris Van Owen

I saw a funny rabbit track,
A stump with snow upon its back,
And then, down where the thistles grow,
Spied fairy footprints in the snow.

I watched the thistle's shadows trace
A lovely pattern made of lace,
And, sparkling in the sun's faint glow,
The tiny footprints in the snow.

Where the road enters the wood,
For a long, long while I stood,
Wondering where the fairies go
Who make the footprints in the snow.

I saw a black-capped chickadee
Who tipped his head and winked at me—
I wonder if they let him know
When they frolic in the snow.

Photo Opposite
SNOWY ADVENTURE
Original art by Donald Zolan
© Pemberton & Oakes—All Rights Reserved

# Small Boy Dilemma

Margaret Freer

I bought this fancy valentine
With lots of lace and stuff.
Hearts and flowers all over
And a verse that's sweet enough
To capture any girl in class
And make her mine forever,
But I'm not sure, at ten years old,
Which girl I think most clever!

Some days I think it's Mary Jane,
Some days I think it's Sue;
Some days I look at Amy Jo,
And then there's Nancy too.
How's a fella' gonna know
Which one of these to pick?
Valentine's Day is coming soon,
And I've got to choose one quick!

Since I've made this big investment
In roses, lace, and rhyme,
I've got to find a girl that's worth
My quarter and my time.
I'll close my eyes and picture
The one who fits the frame,
But just to play it safely,
I don't think I'll sign my name!

# Old-fashioned Valentines

Georgia B. Adams

I like old-fashioned valentines
With lots and lots of lace,
A shy boy in blue knickers, and
A girl with doll-like face.

I like the old inscriptions, like
"Be mine, my Valentine."
I like old-fashioned valentines;
There's love in every line.

And each one has a cupid tucked
Away somewhere, you see;
They've done it for so many years,
Dates to antiquity.

I like old-fashioned valentines!
They seem so warm and true,
And anyway, I guess I am
A bit old-fashioned too!

Photo Opposite
OLD-FASHIONED VALENTINES
Ina Mackey, Photographer

# Handmade Heirloom

## The Intricate Art of Tatting

### Heidi King

Tucked between pillow cases and table-cloths within your linen closet, or perhaps lying underneath a child's christening gown in your antique cedar chest, is most likely an heirloom garment or keepsake linen embel-lished with the centuries-old technique of lace making called tatting. Similar in looks to today's needle art of crochet but much more intricate in design, tatting is primarily used for decorative edgings, insertions, or motifs. Tatting was origi-

nally worked in thick cotton and silk threads, but the introduction of modern cotton and silk threads enabled tatting to evolve into a fashionable way to add beauty and charm to household items, such as guest towels and sheets, and clothing, such as undergarments and dresses.

Tatting is achieved by tying and manipulating a series of knots and loops with a small, oblong shuttle that has pointed ends. The shuttle is moved forward, backward, under, and over a single thread that is loosely attached to the shuttle at one end and wound around a center bobbin at the other. One hand remains relaxed while the other hand holds the thread tightly. The American version of the shuttle has a tiny hook attached to one pointed end for use in drawing threads through small rings called picots.

At first, mastering this intricate art appears to be an arduous task, but after several attempts, it becomes easier and more manageable. Because of the elimination of dozens of bobbins, tatting is easier than lace making and produces much stronger lace more suitable for use on everyday items. Italian women with quick, agile fingers became so proficient in tatting that they nicknamed the art *chiacchierino*, a derivative of the word meaning "to gossip," because the work was easily accomplished while the daily news was exchanged.

The origin of tatting is uncertain. Some experts believe it originated from early Egyptian handiwork, but others assume that the delicate procedure progressed from the ancient maritime techniques of knotting. At any rate, this style of knotted lace spread first to China and then to Europe, where it was named *occhi*, meaning "eyes" in Italian, *frivolite* in France to denote its fragile appearance, and *schiffchenarbeit*, meaning "little boat work" in Germany.

The English word "tatting" is a derivative of tatters, a name for an early form of the modern procedure. The work was fragile and disconnected; all the rings were made separately and later sewn onto fabric in various patterns.

In 1707, the first reference to the English form of tatting was made in a poem called "The Royal Knotter," a tribute to the tatting skills of Queen Mary. Later in the eighteenth century, two paintings also depicted ladies holding tatting shuttles. Throughout the remainder of the century, however, the technique's popularity declined.

It wasn't until the Victorian era in the middle of the nineteenth century that interest in the exquisite craft was renewed. During the 1830s, Mademoiselle Riego of France began writing a number of books on the subject and tremendously improved the existing tatting methods. Considered to be the founder of modern techniques, Riego introduced the foundation chain, which consisted of joining the small picots on the outside of the main chain to form rings and chains within the design, instead of having to sew the work together in patterns once it was finished.

During the early twentieth century, Queen Marie and Lady Hoare, both from Romania, improved tatting's existing techniques and designs. Because they used simple cotton cording to form designs that were similar to intricate bobbin laces, tatting quickly became known as "poor man's lace."

Today, the accessibility of inexpensive trims and the lack of current patterns and literature have turned this ancient craft into a neglected traditional art. Although it is still treasured for its dainty and elegant patterns, most of today's tatting is found displayed or stored with other family heirlooms—treasures that were affectionately handmade years earlier by an older loved one.

# Paper Heart

Sue Lennon

A heart made out of paper
Means the world to me.
It's pasted on cardboard
As crooked as can be.

But when it comes from someone
As dear to me as you,
It doesn't even matter
If it's sticky from the glue.

Just to know you made it
Especially for me,
I'm proud to put it on my desk
For all the world to see.

I may get other valentines
But none that will compare
With a heart made out of paper
And glued with loving care.

Photo Opposite
HOMEMADE VALENTINE
Dietrich Photography

# Bits & Pieces

Yet love, mere love, is beautiful indeed,
And worthy of acceptation.

Elizabeth Barrett Browning

I think we had the chief of all love's joys
Only in knowing that we love each other.

George Eliot

All thoughts, all passions, all delights,
Whatever stirs this mortal frame,
All are but ministers of Love,
And feed his sacred flame.

Samuel Taylor Coleridge

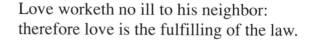

Love worketh no ill to his neighbor:
therefore love is the fulfilling of the law.

Romans 13:10

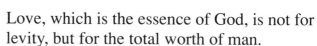

Love, which is the essence of God, is not for
levity, but for the total worth of man.

Ralph Waldo Emerson

I love her with a love as still
As a broad river's peaceful might,
Which, by high tower and lowly mill,
Goes wandering at its own will,
And yet doth ever flow aright.

James Russell Lowell


The presence of those we love makes us
compassionate and generous.

Henry Wadsworth Longfellow


Love is sweet
Given or returned. Common as light is love,
And its familiar voice wearies not ever.

Percy Bysshe Shelley


Love is an image of God, and not a lifeless
image, but the living essence of the divine
nature which beams full of all goodness.

Martin Luther


My heart is like a singing bird
Whose nest is in a watered shoot;
My heart is like an apple-tree
Whose boughs are bent with thick-set fruit;
My heart is like a rainbow shell
That paddles in a halcyon sea;
My heart is gladder than all these
Because my love is come to me.

Christina Rossetti

# To Be in Love with You

Garnett Ann Schultz

It's nice to be in love with you,
So nice to know you care,
To treasure all the happiness
That you and I can share.
A shining dream at last comes true
To know your wondrous worth,
The bit of heaven sweet and dear
You bring me here on earth.

It's nice to know you think of me,
That smiles can be our own,
That life is filled with tender warmth,
That we'll never be alone.
To ever know the beautiful,
The moon and stars on high,
While hand in hand we walk our road
As days and years go by.

It's nice to be in love with you
As you're in love with me.
When someone cares, it helps us know
How precious life can be.
The sweetest dream is sweeter still
When it is shared by two.
That's why it is so very nice
To be in love with you.

Photo Opposite
VALENTINE TREASURES
Gerald Koser

Love me as I love,
Give thy heart for mine,
And trust for evermore
Thy faithful
Valentine.

A Token of Love

# A
# SLICE OF LIFE

Edgar A. Guest

## A Cup of Tea

Nellie made a cup of tea,
Made and poured it out for me,
And above the steaming brew
Smiled and asked me: "One or two?"
Saucily she tossed her head,
"Make it sweet for me," I said.

Two sweet lumps of sugar fell
Into that small china well,
But I knew the while I drained
Every drop the cup contained,
More than sugar in the tea
Made the beverage sweet for me.

This to her I tried to say
In that golden yesterday—
Life is like a cup of tea
Which Time poureth endlessly,
Brewed by trial's constant heat,
Needing love to make it sweet.

Then I caught her looking up,
And I held my dainty cup
Out to her and bravely said:
"Here is all that lies ahead,
Here is all my life to be—
Will you make it sweet for me?"

That was years ago, and now
There is silver in her brow;
We have sorrowed, we have smiled,
We've been hurt and reconciled—
But whatever had to be,
She has made it sweet for me.

---

*Edgar A. Guest began his illustrious career in 1895 at the age of fourteen when his work first appeared in the* Detroit Free Press. *His column was syndicated in over 300 newspapers, and he became known as "The Poet of the People."*

# Valentine Recipe

Georgia B. Adams

Take lots of love and sentiment,
Mix well with bits of cheer,
Add liberally kind thoughts and deeds
Each day throughout the year.

Stir in a kiss, a warm embrace;
And when that special day
Called Valentine's comes 'round again
In a warm and heartfelt way,

Send her a lacy valentine
That speaks your love to her;
This recipe is sure to please,
Just add each one and stir.

This recipe is tried and true;
Just try it and you'll see
Why I believe that true love needs
This faultless recipe!

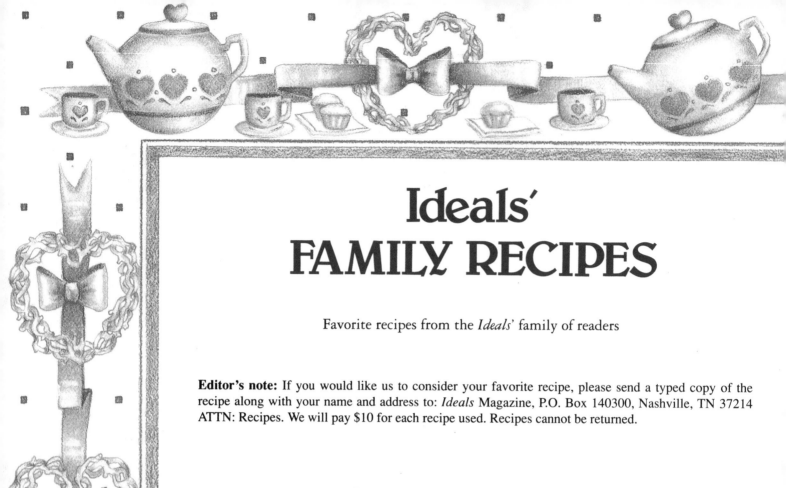

# Ideals'
# FAMILY RECIPES

*Favorite recipes from the* Ideals' *family of readers*

**Editor's note:** If you would like us to consider your favorite recipe, please send a typed copy of the recipe along with your name and address to: *Ideals* Magazine, P.O. Box 140300, Nashville, TN 37214 ATTN: Recipes. We will pay $10 for each recipe used. Recipes cannot be returned.

## MAPLE PECAN MUFFINS

Preheat oven to 400°. Grease or line twenty-four 2½-inch muffin cups and set aside. In a large mixing bowl, stir together 3 cups of all-purpose flour, 1 cup of whole wheat flour, 3 teaspoons of baking powder, 1 teaspoon of baking soda, and ½ teaspoon of salt. Make a well in the center of the dry mixture and set aside.

In a second mixing bowl, combine 2 beaten eggs, 1½ cups of milk, ⅔ cup of vegetable oil, and ⅔ cup of pure maple syrup. Add egg mixture all at once to flour mixture and stir until batter is just moistened (it should remain lumpy). Fold in 1 cup of chopped pecans.

Spoon batter into the greased muffin cups; fill each cup ⅔ full. Bake in preheated 400° oven for 20 minutes or until done (cooking time may vary slightly). Remove muffins from cups and place them on a wire rack to cool.

In a small bowl, mix 1 cup of sifted powdered sugar, 2 tablespoons of maple syrup, and 2 teaspoons of water. Drizzle maple glaze over muffins. Makes two dozen.

Kathleen Marie
Richmond, Virginia

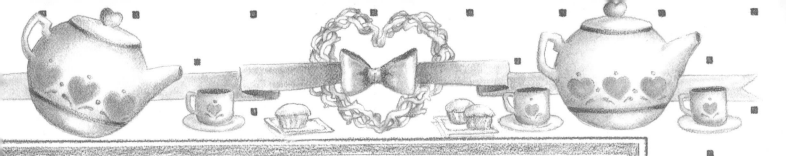

## CRANBERRY-NUT MUFFINS

Preheat oven to 375°. Grease or line one dozen 2½-inch muffin cups and set aside. In a large mixing bowl, combine ¼ cup of shortening, 3 tablespoons of sugar, and 1 egg; blend well. Add ¾ cup of chopped cranberries, ½ cup of chopped walnuts, and 1 teaspoon of grated orange peel to mixture and mix well.

In a second mixing bowl, combine 2 cups of flour and ½ teaspoon of salt. Add half of flour mixture and 1 cup of milk to mixture of cranberries and shortening. Mix well; add remaining flour mixture. Mix all ingredients well.

Spoon batter into the greased muffin cups; fill each cup ⅔ full. Bake in preheated 375° oven for 20 minutes or until done (cooking time may vary slightly). Remove muffins from cups and place them on a wire rack. Allow muffins to cool slightly before serving. Makes one dozen.

Teri Zweifel
Nashville, Tennessee

## OATMEAL CHERRY MUFFINS

Preheat oven to 350°. Grease or line sixteen 2½-inch muffin cups and set aside. In a mixing bowl, whisk together 1½ cups of all-purpose flour, 1 tablespoon of baking powder, and ¾ teaspoon of salt. Add ¾ cup of old-fashioned oats to flour mixture and set aside.

In a second bowl, toss ½ cup of finely chopped walnuts and ½ cup of dried, pitted cherries (or raisins) with 1 teaspoon of flour mixture. In a third mixing bowl, combine 3 tablespoons of softened butter, 1 egg, ¾ cup of firmly packed light-brown sugar, and ¾ cup of milk; beat together. Add egg mixture to flour mixture, stirring until batter is evenly moistened. Fold in cherry-nut mixture.

Spoon batter into the prepared muffin cups; fill each ¾ full. Bake in preheated 350° oven for 20 minutes or until done (cooking time may vary slightly). Remove muffins from muffin cups and place them on a wire rack to cool slightly. Muffins are best when served warm. Makes sixteen.

Cathy Odom
Richardson, Texas

# Brave Love

Author Unknown

He'd nothing but his violin,
I'd nothing but my song;
But we were wed when skies were blue
And summer days were long.
And when we rested by the hedge,
The robins came and told
How they had dared to woo and win
When early spring was cold.

We sometimes supped on dewberries
Or slept among the hay,
But oft the farmers' wives at eve
Came out to hear us play
The rare old tunes, the dear old tunes.
We could not starve for long
While my man had his violin
And I my sweet love song.

The world has gone well with us,
Dear man, since we are one.
Our carefree wandering down the lanes,
It long ago was done.
But those who wait for gold or gear,
For houses and for kine,
Till youth's sweet spring grows brown and sere,
And love and beauty tine,
Will never know the joy of hearts
That met without a fear,
When you had but your violin
And I a song, my dear.

Photo Opposite
ROSES AND SHEET MUSIC
Ina Mackey, Photographer

# TO
# MY HUSBAND

Garnett Ann Schultz

To my husband, brave and bold,
This is what the message told:
Nothing fancy, nothing fine,
Only one small valentine.

Just a kiss and just a smile,
All to make your life worthwhile,
Proud that you have shared my life:
To my husband—from your wife.

# TO
# MY WIFE

Garnett Ann Schultz

Bits of ribbon, bits of lace,
Hearts and flowers all in place,
Tender love words, sweet and dear,
Bringing you a world of cheer.

Hope and courage from above,
These I bring you with my love,
For you, dearest, sweetheart mine,
To my wife—my valentine.

# Rose of Love

Douglas Malloch

A rose within a crystal glass,
A rose to wither and to pass;
Its beauty fades, its glory goes,
I know no way to keep a rose.

And yet there is a rose that blooms
Forevermore in quiet rooms,
A rose within a fairer vase
Than purchased in the market place.

The rose is love, the vase the home,
A rose that blossoms when we roam,
And when return, one rose God made
That need not wither, need not fade.

And yet to keep that one rose fair,
The heart must also give it care,
Must nurture it with things like this:
The morning smile, the goodnight kiss.

Aye, this is all the red rose needs:
Words of affection, helpful deeds,
Labors divided, burdens shared,
And eyes that look as though they cared.

If you the rose of love possess,
Keep it alive with tenderness,
And crystal pure with gentle hands
The vase called home in which it stands.

There is one rose, the rose of love,
You need not know the fading of,
A rose that, watered day by day,
You never need to throw away.

Photo Opposite
VALENTINE GIFTS
Ina Mackey, Photographer

## How Do I Love Thee?

My mother and father have had a long and loving marriage. They are best friends and soul-mates, sparring partners and comrades-in-arms. They have experienced a world war, financial reversals, business success, and several years of retirement—all with equal grace. One of the reasons they have successfully endured as a couple for almost fifty years is because they have truly learned how to say "I love you."

They learned to say it in all the situations that life presents, in the large and small moments that build a relationship. They taught me what loving really means by example. I never heard my parents call each other names or ridicule one another. Not that there weren't opportunities! Oh, there were times when foolish things were done and poor investments were made, but love was expressed in a willingness to let it pass without recrimination. Perhaps each knew the tables could easily be turned and the merciful one would need forgiveness next time.

Mother's quiet, detail-oriented approach to life must have clashed often with Dad's boisterous, haphazard ways; yet she always seemed to delight in his unique and humorous antics. At a moment's notice, he would remember the lyrics to a ridiculous song he had learned "way back when" and have her doubled over with giggles like a school girl.

I remember the time she spotted a dead tree root that had been sanded and shaped by the surf into a figure resembling a dinosaur. She remarked that it would make an interesting addition to the front of our house at the beach. That afternoon at high tide, Dad marched down the beach, sawed the root from its upended trunk, tied a rope around its "neck," and led his floating trophy back to our beach house. As he waved his saw above his head in triumph, he presented the captured "monster" to my mother much like a knight might deliver a slain dragon to his fair damsel. Twenty years later, the "Treeanasaurus" still stands his pre-historic watch tied securely to the fence surrounding their beach house.

When birthdays and other holidays arrive, my parents spend time determining the perfect gift, not by what is most popular that year, but by what they really know about each other. I'm sure many wives would be mortified to receive two dozen six-foot bean poles and a load of chicken manure for Valentine's Day! Not my mom! The year my parents moved from the city to a house surrounded by two acres of land, Mother was dreaming of finally having enough ground for a decent garden. Dad's gift said, "I understand your dream, and I want to help you make it come true." Isn't that what true love is all about?

Another year, he had a rock delivered to her. It wasn't a diamond or ruby, but a five hundred pound hunk of granite. She had often remarked how lovely it would be to take a cup of coffee outside on a sunny morning and sit basking in the sun on a warm rock. Whenever I'm home on a visit, I often take a cup of coffee and go sit on that rock. To me, it says volumes about the solid foundation of love in our home, a foundation built by two people who learned to say "I love you" in countless ways.

Sometimes the love was spoken in silence, in the ability to refrain from nagging and allow a fault to pass unnoticed. I recall the smile on my mother's face as she listened once again to Dad's retelling a favorite experience or story. He rarely remembered all the details correctly, and dates and locations sometimes shifted with each telling; but she was always his most appreciative audience. I remember asking her once, "Don't you tire of hearing the same stories over and over?" She looked at me indulgently and replied, "I would find it much more tedious to be without his stories, even if I've heard them dozens of times." I didn't understand her answer then, but now I do.

When you love and have been loved, there is nothing sweeter than spending time together; and in a deep love, the times may not always be sweet. Their love has stood the test of serving and helping, of praying and encouraging. Through these times, they discovered new opportunities to say "I love you." When illness robbed Daddy of his appetite, Mother combed the grocery's shelves for appealing treats and woke with him at midnight to fix a cup of cocoa and a warm butterhorn.

My parents would never consider themselves teachers or poets, but my parents have been both to me. When I read "How do I love thee, let me count the ways . . . ," I do not think of Elizabeth Barrett Browning; I think of my mother and dad and of the countless ways they taught me love could be expressed.

---

*Pamela Kennedy is a freelance writer of short stories, articles, essays, and children's books. Married to a naval officer and mother of three children, she has made her home on both U.S. coasts and in Hawaii and currently resides in Washington, D.C. She draws her material from her own experiences and memories, adding bits of her imagination to create a story or mood.*

# Love

Margaret Rorke

Love is a nod from across the room.
    Love is a knowing wink.
Love is a laugh from my heart's full bloom.
    Love is a pause to think
Selflessly, wholly, of what it shares.
    Threaded by man and wife,
Quietly weaving till unaware,
    Love is the whole of life.

Love is an arm to support an arm.
    Love wipes away a tear.
Love speaks of love with a special charm.
    Love is a listening ear.
Love is the squeeze of a gentle hand
    Saying what words can't say.
Knowing such love makes one understand
    God in a wiser way.

Photo Opposite
ANTIQUE WRITING DESK
Roger Smith
Vision Impact Photolibrary

# Quiet Time

Craig E. Sathoff

In evening when the tales are through
And prayers have all been said,
There is a special quiet time,
Our children tucked in bed.

There is a time for wife and me
To ponder at our ease

The tasks that face us day to day
Within our family.

There is a time for hopes and dreams,
A time to look ahead,
A time to count our blessings
And to check our sleepyheads.

There is a time to understand
The goals we face as one.
A simple, quiet, peaceful time
Before the day is done.

# Little Shadows

LaVerne P. Larson

Little shadows o'er the snow
On a frosty day,
Flying, scurrying, seeking food
From winter's cold display.

Sometimes they find a meager meal,
Perhaps a crust of bread;

LITTLE FRIEND
Dianne Dietrich Leis, Photographer

But when I hear their grateful song,
I know they've been well fed.

Little shadows o'er the snow
Are happy when they find
Tiny blessings placed with care
By someone who is kind.

And so it is with life itself;
A smile, word, or deed
May be a blessing bringing joy
To someone's heart in need.

# LEGENDARY AMERICANS

Nancy Skarmeas

## John Bartram

John Bartram's family heritage made him a farmer, but his unique sensitivity to the intricate wonders of the land made him a botanist. This combination made him exceptional; John Bartram not only worked the land to make his living, but he also studied it and nurtured it and respected it. Late in life, Bartram described the moment when John Bartram the farmer became John Bartram the botanist. Resting from his work with a plow, Bartram noticed a single daisy; and taking a moment to study it, he experienced a revelation. "What a shame," he chided himself, "that thou hast spent so many years in the ruthless destroying of that which the Lord in His infinite goodness hath made so perfect in its humble place, without trying to understand one of its simplest leaves." Bartram returned to his plow and to the work of farming, but with a "new desire for inquiry into the perfections the Lord hath granted to us all about." The land was not merely his servant, it became his partner and his teacher.

Born in 1699, John Bartram was raised after his parents' death by his grandparents on their farm in Darby, Pennsylvania. Throughout boyhood, Bartram was interested in botany, but he had very limited access to the literature and formal education in the field. After a few years of schooling, Bartram began work on his grandparents' farm. Ironically, his farming career launched his career in botany.

Through working the fields, Bartram's botanical knowledge was mostly self-taught. He learned through a devoted course of independent reading and his daily interaction with the farmland. In 1728 at age twenty-nine, John Bartram purchased his own farm on the bank of the Schuylkill River. When he bought the farm, it covered slightly more than one hundred acres; through hard work and innovation, he expanded it to three hundred acres and turned a profit every year. After the revelation of the daisy, however, successful farming was never the end for Bartram; it was part of his education, part of his journey toward a better understanding of God's natural world. Although his botanical garden occupied only the long, sloping front lawn of the farm, Bartram referred to all of his property as his "darling garden," and he sought to learn from every plant on every acre.

Bartram found another source of education through his longtime friend and Philadelphia neighbor Benjamin Franklin, who helped the Pennsylvania botanist establish correspondences with several prominent English botanists. From these men, Bartram received information and encouragement; they in turn valued the colonist for his unique perspective on their science. In the late eighteenth century, most botanists in the colonies were occupied with transplanting the plants they had known in Europe to their New World homes. Bartram, however, was devoted to the task of identifying and collecting new native species. His extensive travels throughout the country enabled him to introduce two hundred New World plant species to Europe, including the mountain laurel and the Franklin tree. Bartram very definitely was a student of American botany.

Bartram received another benefit from his exchange of letters with England. As his reputation among British botanists grew, his name came to the attention of King George III, who was impressed enough to name Bartram "Royal Botanist" in 1765. This position paid fifty pounds a year, money that allowed Bartram to extend his travels and expand his collections. After 1765, he settled into a productive routine, working his Schuylkill River farm and garden from mid-spring until fall and travelling in the winter throughout the colonies and eastern Canada collecting plants, seeds, and cuttings to propagate and study on his farm.

Bartram's routine, however, changed drastically as increasing hostilities between the American colonies and England eventually escalated into the Revolutionary War. He lost his stipend as "Royal Botanist" and many of his contacts in England, but Bartram worried more about the safety and preservation of his garden. Although Bartram wanted no part of the conflict that threatened his life's work, he and his garden could not escape the war.

During the Battle of Brandywine, British General Howe and his troops set up camp on Bartram's farm. To Howe and his men, Bartram's farm was no different from any other place they had pitched their tents; but for reasons unknown, General Howe saw to it that his men left Bartram's land and farmhouse exactly as they had found it.

Bartram did not live to see the conclusion of the Revolutionary War; he died in 1777. Bartram's Garden, however, survived the war, and its variety and prosperity attracted scientists and tourists eager to see the natural paradise on the banks of the Schuylkill River. Today, the garden survives as the oldest botanical garden in the United States, and John Bartram, the farmer who cared more for his work with plants than for profits or politics, is remembered as the father of American botany.

# February Says Good-bye

Blanche McCauley Hallett

February says good-bye
With a teardrop in her eye
And a blanket white to cover
All the winter's bare spots over.

First she dusts the bushes well;
Then she rests herself a spell
And turns the sunshine on to see
The kind of picture this will be.

Then she sends the snow in showers
To make her own bouquet of flowers
Before the spring is ushered in
And she must say goodbye again.

# TRAVELER'S
## *Diary*

Tim Hamling

© Tom Bernard

## Historic Bartram's Garden

Historic Bartram's Garden lies just northwest of the banks of the Schuylkill River in southwest Philadelphia. On this site more than two hundred and fifty years ago, John Bartram laid the foundations for the country's oldest surviving botanical garden. Today, the garden's meticulous preservation and natural beauty invite all to explore the natural wonders that lured John Bartram from his career as farmer to become America's first great botanist and naturalist.

A walk along aptly named Azalea Way from the riverbank to the preserved Bartram House reveals a few of the garden's riches. Native species of rhododendron and mountain laurel collected by Bartram and his son William on their travels line the shaded path. Species of willow oak, pawpaw, flame azalea, highbush blueberry, bur oak, and shagbark hickory add to the variety. Also along the path is the famed *Franklinia*, a species discovered by John and William Bartram on a trip to Georgia in 1765 and perhaps Bartram's most famous discovery. Named in honor of Bartram's friend Benjamin Franklin, the tree could not be found in the wild after 1803. All *Franklinias* growing today are descended from those propagated by John and William Bartram. They are credited with saving it from extinction.

Closer to the Bartram House are some smaller, more specialized gardens. A kitchen garden containing a wide variety of herbs and vegetables that Bartram grew for culinary, medicinal, and domestic uses grows next to a flower garden where Bartram tended the plants and bulbs that he traded with other botanists. This method of exchange enabled Bartram to add great variety to his collection.

Many of the species in Bartram's Garden are of historical as well as botanical interest. The last survivor of the three Ginkgo trees imported to the United States from China grows on Bartram's land. A friend and fellow botanist of William Bartram gave him the tree in the 1780s. On the northwest side of Bartram House is a rare species that is a hybrid of a red and willow oak. The specimen is called Bartram oak in honor of John Bartram, who discovered this species growing on his farm.

Many of the more delicate shrubs and vines in the garden grow next to Bartram House. Along the stone facade on the house's east side are specimens of crossvine, pomegranate, common jujube, common fig, and a Petre pear, a direct descendant of the tree grown from a seed sent to John Bartram by Lady Petre of England in 1739. Like the variety of trees and shrubs in the garden, Bartram House has expanded and prospered since its purchase in 1728.

When Bartram purchased the land that Bartram's Garden now occupies, it contained farmland and a small stone farmhouse, two rooms long and one room wide. The farm exposed Bartram to the plants in his own backyard, and his interest in botany quickly became a passion. In the 1730s, Bartram collected a variety of plants, cuttings, and seeds from the Philadelphia area to plant and cultivate on his farm. By the 1760s, he had travelled throughout the east—north to New York, west to Pittsburgh, and south to Charleston, South Carolina—collecting more plants to study and grow.

In 1770, Bartram expanded the farm house he originally bought with the land. He extended the river facade by the depth of one room and faced it with local stone. He added a two-story portico and a peaked roof as well as ornamental inscriptions and window carvings. When Bartram died in 1777, he left the estate to two of his sons, William and John Jr.

The brothers took advantage of the wide variety of plants, shrubs, and trees and converted the garden into a commercial nursery called John Bartram & Son. In 1783, they published a seed catalog offering seeds, cuttings, and plants for sale. When both brothers died, the house and nursery were left to John Jr.'s daughter, Ann Bartram Carr. She and her husband expanded both the nursery and the house but were forced to sell the property in 1850 due to financial difficulties.

The property was purchased by a successful Philadlphia businessman, Andrew Eastwick, who transformed the nursery into a pleasure garden for his family and friends. Eastwick enlisted his gardener, Thomas Meehan, to catalog all the species of plants, shrubs, and trees in the garden. Eastwick's and Meehan's meticulous care and appreciation for the garden are greatly responsible for the garden's current preservation.

The property remained in the Eastwick family until it was bought by the city of Philadelphia in 1891. In 1893, descendants of John Bartram founded the John Bartram Association to assist the city in preserving the beauty and variety of the garden. The association's programs expose visitors to the wide variety of plants and trees in the garden as well as the techniques and lifestyle of a colonial gardener. Most importantly, the preservation of Historic Bartram's Garden enables any visitor to share John Bartram's passion and appreciation for the beauty and variety of the natural world.

# Seasons Yet To Come

Fay Mofield

When winter time is gloomy
And snow is all around,
Pray to God for eyes to see
The beauty beneath the ground.

The little seeds that wait to grow
And the animals that sleep
Are waiting for the sun to warm
And wake them from the deep.

The golden rays will melt the snow
And thaw the frozen ground.
Every season has to change;
Not one will stay around.

So give thanks to God for seasons past
And seasons yet to come.
Remember God is in everything;
His hand is on everyone.

Photo Opposite
BLOOMING CROCUS
Kevin Shields/New England Stock Photo

Deana Deck

## Catalog Dreaming

There's a cheap, quick shortcut to summer that's good to keep in mind during this frigid season known as midwinter. It comes in the mailbox, costs little or nothing, and is good for several hours of "summertime state of mind." Of course, I'm referring to the plethora of seed catalogs that begin to arrive just after the holidays. If you don't receive any now, it's easy to get on the list. Just order any one of them and you'll soon be inundated with samples of all the rest. Nobody shares mailing lists like the seed companies!

I encountered my first seed catalogs when I was about seven. My grandfather was raised on a wheat farm, but he moved into the city as a young man and entered the lumber business. In his heart, he was forever a farmer, and throughout his life, he always owned some land out in the country. In our family, it was known as "Grandpa's Ten Acres." There, with the help of a tenant farmer, he raised a few animals and kept a large vegetable garden and a vast cornfield. Those rows of vegetables held many wonderfully fragrant hiding places for a small child.

On winter evenings, he would sit in his favorite chair by the radio and browse through the seed catalogs that had arrived by the dozens. I would sit on his lap as he read the descriptions to me. I was just learning to read and was fascinated by books of any kind, but what riveted my attention to the seed catalogs were the incredible photographs. The colorful pictures of huge, juicy red tomatoes would make my mouth water—and I didn't even like tomatoes! The corn seemed to glisten with butter—or was it just the dew? The watermelons looked succulent and sweet, the radishes crisp and cold.

The flower seed sections were breathtaking—gigantic "State Fair" zinnias, brilliant marigolds, and dramatic morning glories. The petunias were always pictured in a vast array of colors with large, perfectly formed blooms, unlike the scraggly ones in our backyard.

The finest catalogs, my very favorites, were those sent by the fruit tree nurseries. Their covers were always graced by huge golden peaches or ripe red apples. Inside were mounds of rasberries, cherries, and blackberries and bushel baskets filled with pears, plums, and bunches of grapes. These winter evening sessions always aroused such a craving for fresh fruit that my grandfather would eventually send me to the kitchen for some apples. I'd watch him peel and core them and cut them in "wagon wheels"; and, as we devoured them one by one, we would plan the paradise we imagined as our next summer's garden. Despite my grandmother's admonitions to "remember last year," we invariably ordered too many seeds.

I still revel in the piles of catalogs that arrive in early January, and I still order too many seeds. The best known catalogs for vegetables are from Park Seed Company and W.E. Burpee. Both also offer small fruits and garden supplies. Less well known, but equally good, is Henry Field's Seed and Nursery catalog. It includes not only vegetables and fruits, but also many grass seed varieties, shade trees, ornamentals, and hedges.

My favorite catalog for flowers is the gorgeous offering from White Flower Farm. Their plant descriptions make excellent reading and are packed with helpful cultivation tips. The Klehm Nursery in Illinois sends a wonderful perennial catalog that includes a large selection on ornamental grasses. If you like clematis, don't miss the specialized catalog from Arthur H. Steffen's Clematis. The Jackson & Perkins catalog is the one to have if you want to daydream about roses, and the Lilypons catalog is a must if you have even the slightest interest in water gardens.

For unusual varieties of flower seeds, the colorful Thompson & Morgan catalog is a must. To give you an idea of its scope, it offers forty-eight different varieties of bluebells! Shepherd's Garden Seeds catalog has many herbs, perennials, and old-fashioned annuals. This catalog lacks color photographs, but each page offers a delicately hand-drawn sketch that makes up for it.

If you're going to spend the winter daydreaming about your garden, you may as well daydream about the tools for making your garden tasks a pleasurable experience. There are two "wishbooks" that are essential additions to the serious garden dreamer's catalog collection. One is the Smith & Hawkins catalog, and the other is the incomparable Gardener's Eden catalog.

I have only listed a few of my favorites here, but there are literally thousands of others available. Finding them is easy if you have a copy of the catalog of catalogs. It's called *Gardening by Mail* and is cross-indexed by plant, subject matter, and other categories to make it easy to locate the catalog you need.

Most seed catalogs are free. The ones that aren't, like White Flower Farm's offering, will usually deduct the cost of the catalog from your first order. To remain on the nurseries' mailing lists, you eventually need to purchase something. A few nurseries have minimum order requirements, but these are rare. Most nurseries base their shipping charges on the amount of the order. The more you order, the less the shipping charge. If you make a purchase, you automatically receive the next year's catalog; but the catalogs are expensive to print, so most companies purge their lists frequently and will delete your name if you stop buying.

A word of warning—once you get involved in the game of catalog dreaming, you might need to enlarge your land holdings. I find that my garden fills up quickly every year, and I have developed a clearer understanding about why my grandfather needed ten acres to accommodate his "garden patch."

*Deana Deck lives in Nashville, Tennessee, where her garden column is a regular feature in the* The Tennessean.

# Readers' Forum

———— ———— ———— ———— ———— ————

Today I received a copy of *Ideals* and wish to thank you ever so much for it is indeed a splendid magazine. I am enjoying the photography and poems more than I can tell you. . . . I will share the copy with friends. Thank you again for the joy it has given me.

Norma Brewer
Mountain View, California

I bought my first *Ideals* book at Christmas 1977. Since then I've always had a subscription to *Ideals*. I have kept every issue and reread them all the time. Keep up the wonderful work. *Ideals* is the BEST.

Mrs. Francis Simon
St. Cloud, Minnesota

I received my copy of *Ideals* yesterday and started reading it. Now that I am well into it I had to stop and write this letter to you telling you what a wonderful and great book it is. . . . My family and I really enjoy *Ideals* magazine. I really look forward to each one.

Jack Clanton
Shreveport, Louisiana

Statement of ownership, management, and circulation (Required by 39 U.S.C. 3685), of Ideals, published eight times a year in February, March, May, June, August, September, November, and December at Nashville, Tennessee, for September 1992. Publisher, Patricia A. Pingry; Editor, Tim Hamling; Managing Editor, as above; Owner, Egmont U.S., Inc., wholly owned subsidiary of The Egmont Foundation, VOGNMAGERGADE 11, 1148 Copenhagen, K, Denmark. The known bondholders, mortgages, and other securities are: None. Average no. copies each issue during preceding 12 months: Total no. copies printed (Net Press Run) 214,688. Paid circulation 37,244. Mail subscription 157,693. Total paid circulation 194,937. Free distribution 828. Total distribution 195,765. Actual no. copies of single issue published nearest to filing date: Total no. copies printed (Net Press Run) 170,061. Paid circulation 10,053. Mail subscription 145,066. Total paid circulation 155,119. Free distribution 361. Total distribution 155,480. I certify that the statements made by me above are correct and complete. Rose A. Yates, Vice President, Direct Marketing Systems and Operations.

———— ———— ———— ———— ———— ————

## ADDRESSES FOR *CATALOG DREAMING*

Park Seed Company, Cokesbury Road, Greenwood, SC 29647-0001
W.A. Burpee Co., 300 Park Avenue, Warminster, PA 18991-0001
Henry Field's Seed & Nursery Co., 415 North Burnett, Shenandoah, IA 51602
White Flower Farm, Litchfield, CT 06759-0050
Klehm Nursery, Box 197 Penny Road, Route 5, South Barrington, IL 60010-9555
Arthur H. Steffen, Inc., 1259 Fairport Road, P.O. Box 184, Fairport, NY 14450
Jackson & Perkins, 2518 South Pacific Highway, Medford, OR 97501
Lilypons Water Gardens, 6800 Lilypons Road, P.O. Box 10, Lilypons, MD 21717-0010
Thompson & Morgan, Inc., P.O. Box 1308, Jackson, NJ 08527
Shepherd's Garden Seeds, 6116 Highway 9, Felton, CA 95018
Smith & Hawkins, 25 Corte Madera, Mill Valley, CA 94941
Gardener's Eden, P.O. Box 7307, San Francisco, CA 94120-7307
*Gardening By Mail—A Source Book* by Barbara J. Barton, Tusker Press, P.O. Box 1338, Sebastopol, CA 95473